MW00453778

this boy is a constellation

sam payne

this boy is a constellation
Copyright © 2020 Sam Payne
www.bysampayne.com

All rights reserved.

No part of this book may be reproduced in whole or in part, or stored in a retrieval system, or trans-
mitted in any form or by any means, electronic, mechanical, photocopying, scanning, recording, or
otherwise without permission from the writer or publisher.

First edition.

ISBN-13: 9781076397201

for mum and dad—
you kept my stars aligned
when i started to waver.

for the readers—
you set my skies alight
with your strength and kindness.

and finally for him—
you showed me how to love again.

for mum and dad—
you kept my stars aligned
when i started to waver.

for the readers—
you set my skies alight
with your strength and kindness.

and finally for him—
you showed me how to love again.

contents

when midnight came

he was winter—
crumpling my leaves
swallowing all my colour
draining stars from my sky

you could almost hear me
nervously holding a breath
as my stem snapped
under his step

(*in the dead of night*)

i was a garden to treasure
not a harvest to reap

you deflowered me anyway
plucked me petal from stem

tugged me trunk from earth
until my soil was barren

(*my wilds were destroyed*)

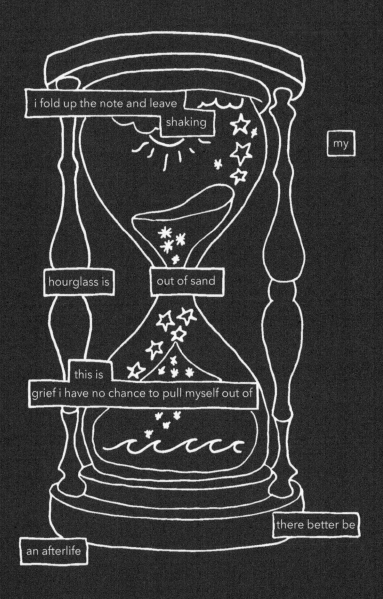

i fold up the note and leave

shaking

my

hourglass is   out of sand

this is

grief i have no chance to pull myself out of

there better be

an afterlife

when you question
whether he is worthy
of your love
remember
he shook your roots
and made leaves
f
  a
    l
      l
        from your branches

(*the shake down*)

<u>firsts and lasts:</u>
- those lips in the park on that day.
- that pain in my chest two years later.
- those hands in my sheets that september.
- the same hands, hungry for lust not love.
- those tears of joy on our cheeks.
- the sea of tears i cried that winter.
- three words written on that green note.
- waiting for those words to be repeated back.
  one. last. time.

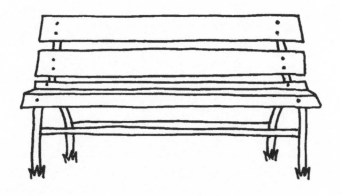

there are still days i wake
creased by memories of you

the taste of your body
words dripping from your lips

then a fist through my chest
and my soul bleeding out

(*ptsd*)

we may have
the same skin
between our legs
but that doesn't mean
we can't hurt each other
we can't tear each other
limb from limb

(*abuse is genderless*)

after everything you did
it is your words i go back to

'you is smart
you is kind
you is important'

and i wonder if i will ever hear
those words whispered to me again

(*delicate*)

<u>places i find your ghost:</u>
- the blueberry cheesecake. the bridge. the bench where we gazed through leafless branches at the moon.
- my copy of 'the fault in our stars.' your tears still stain the pages.
- the park where we laid under the tree. our eyes met then, our lips met later.
- 'a drop in the ocean' by ron pope. my guitar. you on the edge of my bed.
- the memories in a box, in a bag, behind a door. i'm waiting for them to disappear.

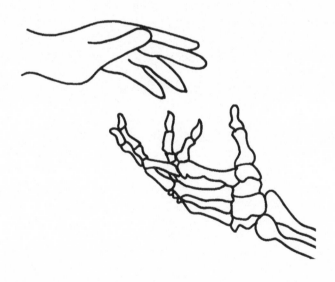

i think of the letters
we scratched into the metal
handrail of that bridge

i wonder if they are still there
i wonder if they survived
what we could not

(*the last piece of us*)

i stood there, looking at

the shore-line
half-closed my

everything i'd

eyes and imagined
ever lost

washed up

on the horizon

he'd

wave, maybe even call

my heart calls out to him
across a turbulent ocean
through fields of gun fire

i am the wind, ruffling his hair
whistling delicately in his ear
'come back to me, love, come back'

(*reunion*)

will someone see
i am not just a tool
to survive lonely nights
but e v e r y t h i n g
they will ever need?

(*i am more*)

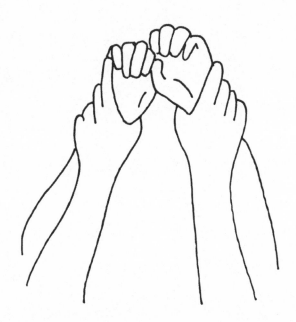

<u>soap will never wash away:</u>
- your fingertips, embossed in the fabric of my skin, each cell remembers you.
- the life you gave me and just as quickly ripped away.
- lifetimes i wasted on dreams we made that will never be. i am trying to shake them off.
- the bravery i found when i locked the door between our worlds and fed the key to the sea.
- my strength. my resilience. me.

the blue tshirt i slept in for a year, then gave to you to remember me by. the guilty flowers. your last minute attempt at sorry. they shrivelled up like my tired heart. the memories and dreams i shook from myself that winter. a river of stardust in my wake. my laughter, trapped in the cold, damp edge of a gutter somewhere, longing to be heard again...

I LEFT THEM BEHIND

they say it takes seven years
to be free of his touch but
i am impatient—

i am shedding this skin
one smothered by
his mouth
his tongue
his hands
and i am growing a new one
baby soft and unscathed

he will not recognise me now
my skin
my power
my voice
will not pollute me
with a single touch

(*touch*)

THINGS I SHOULDN'T HAVE SAID:

'this doesn't have to be over.'

it already was.

'we'll never be friends.'

maybe someday we will.

'you'll never understand this knotted mind of mine.'

you were the only one who did.

'he means nothing to me.'

he always will.

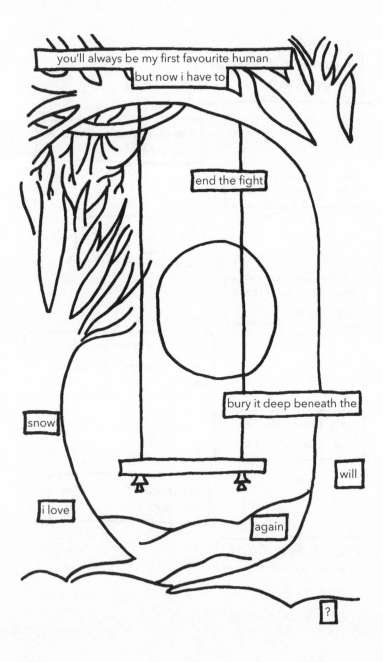

he wandered, a lonely moon

he was the moon, wandering
a timeless path around the earth
as every moon had done before

he never veered far away—
there were stargazers to please
uneasy footsteps to guide home

yet he dreamed of floating away
from expectations and routine
to paint a path of his own making

perhaps he would find another moon
to share a cosy place amongst the stars

(*finding himself*)

i am a victim of this generation
with grades that determine self-worth
clothes that determine social status

with bodies which are devoured
by silent eyes on social media
girls frantically squatting
to feel a little more beautiful
while others are told to 'cover up'
because they are U.G.L.Y.

ugly like the word FAT
ugly like the stretch marks
on a pregnant mother's belly
ugly like the girl with bulimia
who eats three meals a day
just to vomit them back up

and boys who don't cry
because 'masculinity' tells them
that tears aren't brave or strong

a generation that turns to pills
and booze to finally feel free
because we are suffocated by
expectations

do you ever feel so lost
that your mind circles itself
round and round and round and—

you choke on the same memories
of when you were buried alive
by the suffocating night

(*i call this depression*)

onest, too open, too ME?

a lost cause...

BIG plans for f — WHERE did all go? ~

TO FEEL A LITTLE BIT BETTER?

don't try to take her away from me — she's all i have

GIVE UP

I'M NO FUN ANYMORE

i j

n't s with this rling ound y head?

even the simple things are dark blue today

d my achievements in blankets

I'M SO AWKWARD. CRAZY...

because i d

i LOOK IN THE MIRROR AND DON'T KNO

I LOOK

N'T KN

WHY AM I LIKE THIS?

i SWEAR

i'm slowly starting to believe dreams

don't come true like they do in books

i'm so tired of this

WILL THIS ALL JUST END IN DISASTER?

WHEN WILL

is there a reason you decided that turning into a ghast was BETTER THAN saying you wanted to leave?

RITY

what if this is the shower

i'm going to drown

is there out there?

is there anyone

AM I

A MONSTER?

JUST LIKE HIM?

why do ou leave my essages waiting a reply that never arrives?

EARTH, YOU INSPIRED ME TO DO THE SAME

OH!

feel i deserve them

WHO IT IS I SEE!
WHO IT IS I SEE!

i think i'm a little scared to unglue myself from the place beside him

HELP?!

and i can feel myself spiralling
and i can feel myself
and i can feel myself spiralling again

don't deserve this

IS THIS-LIFE-NOW?

HHHH

a good person? is there so DOES NOBODY WANT ME?
NOBODY
NOBODY

SIGH

ng i did

WHY DO

the pain is all too loud and BLINDING

i'm twenty-six years old in just nine months
a reminder that i'm running on borrowed time
as if where i am and where i should be don't align
at least, not in their eyes, the one's that scorn and
say silent things like 'what a waste' and 'run faster'
and 'where is your real job?' and 'who do you love?'
and 'why haven't you figure any of this out yet?'
when i'm dying to reply, 'who has?'

i'm twenty-six years old in just nine months
for the last two decades i've been a studious pupil
followed what to say to make them smile
nodded along politely to their bigotry
worn what's 'masculine' and never painted a nail
so they don't look twice and everything is neat
and everything is as it should be

i'm twenty-six years old in just nine months
won't you just give me some space to breathe?

(*countdown*)

they say,
'you're too thin'
but all i hear is
not enough
not enough
not enough

(*i will be enough for someone*)

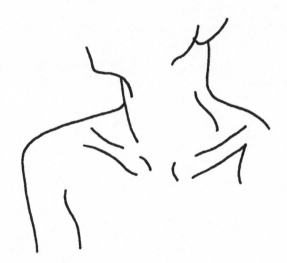

<u>when i began to spiral:</u>
- i stood in the middle of a grass field and admired the sunset alone.
- i learnt to play early 2000s love songs on guitar because nothing sounds better.
- i befriended the cast of queer eye (they don't know it yet, i just love the show).
- i ate way too many biscuits.
- i looked at myself in the mirror and thought about the things i wish i could change.
- i seriously considered getting a piercing.
- i dreamt about the unlikely possibility of finding a boy who loves me in return.
- i tried filling my lungs with fresh air, but choked on the toxic fumes he left behind.
- i talked to people who helped me realise your mind doesn't have to destroy you.
- i wrote a lot of poems about a lot of feelings. this is my release.

i hid away
within myself
for far too long
calling it lost
when i was
simply too scared
to be found

(*i am found*)

my mind is like a banana
each week it starts green
with naivety and optimism

soon it's softened and bruised
pushed down and rotting
at the bottom of the fruit bowl

but here's my secret—
this is when i'm sweetest

(*life in the fruit bowl*)

(this haunted body)

<u>where my mind goes in autumn:</u>
- it falls with the fiery leaves in the sky, back to delicate visions of us falling apart.
- it burns with the memory of our final dance and walking you home in the golden daylight.
- it shivers in the bitter breeze, a chill that once froze tears on these cheeks.
- it tries to run from the grief you shackled to me.
- it brightens in the crisp, white sun. it gave me these words and scorched the pain away.

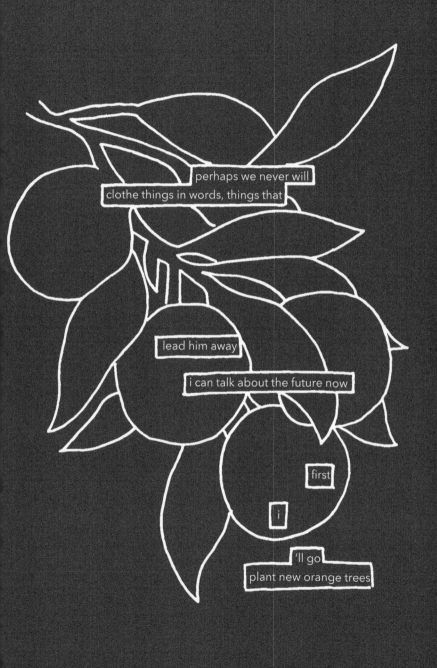

perhaps we never will
clothe things in words, things that

lead him away

i can talk about the future now

first

i

'll go
plant new orange trees

i am afraid to love
for the possibility of
one boy ruining me
the way he did
over and over
and over again

(*catch me when i fall*)

we are all
m i g r a n t s
travelling from
city to city
lover to lover
searching for
home

(*will we find it?*)

new boys came along
and tried me on for size
like a ring they knew
they could admire
but wouldn't keep

(*broken promises*)

he scrolls through faces on his phone
shopping for one that he'd like to love ·

manufactured profiles that feel fake fake fake
hobbies and witty jokes and beach shots
where a guy can be anyone he wants to be

he's taught to fall for a photo without
touching their fingers or hearing their voice

and swapping nudes is the route to a heart
but he'll be lucky if this road isn't a dead-end

(*modern love*)

if a boy wants
to touch you
let him with
his mind first
not his hands

(*they are not worthy*)

when i say
'i feel ugly today'
what i mean is
'nobody has told me
i am beautiful'

(*words matter*)

you are a boy who
happens to like boys

you aren't obliged to
wear flamboyance or
pumped up biceps

these things are not
the rent you pay
to occupy the label 'gay'

these things are not
the rent you pay
to be loveable

(*unless you want to*)

the water tickles my toes
just as your eyes tickle mine
enough to entice me but
not enough to make me stay

(*oh show me how*)

his heartbeat is
an old chorus
a delicate
ocean
around my ankles
eyes a paler green
beautiful. loving. murderous.

he housed a terrifying
passion in his eyes—
a look that could fill
you with sweetness
but just as easily
tear you apart

(*which will it be?*)

i presented myself, naked
swallowed him into my sea

i hoped we could wash up
on a beach beside each other

he took one look
and ran

(*the runaway*)

after we said goodbye
i knew i felt too much

encouraged myself to
think, 'this won't work
you're better alone'

as if isolation was
my heart's desire

(*the first date*)

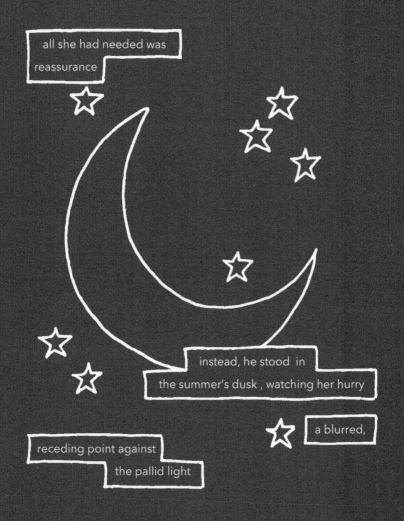

all she had needed was

reassurance

instead, he stood in
the summer's dusk , watching her hurry

a blurred,

receding point against
the pallid light

i'm giddy under your gaze
my lips put on their best show
trying to make you laugh along
but i've been too numb for too long
to know if it means anything or
if i'm playing this show on autopilot

(*is this real or just a show?*)

i knew you wanted to kiss me
felt it as you shuffled towards
my every shuffle away

i wanted to say,
'it isn't intentional,
and in truth, i'm scared'

but i had no time for words
no time to question your lips
as you pulled me in

and i waited for a spark
waited, yet it never came

(*you are worth more than my doubts*)

i want to believe the universe
has my story charted across the sky
that it is fighting to bring me to him

when we collide, he will know
i was always meant to be there
as constant as the moon in the night

(*i don't know him yet*)

i am waiting for
the one who says
'your heart will
be safe here
in my hands'

(*guardian angel*)

<u>things that go away and come back:</u>
- waves. like the sea, your worry comes and goes.
- love. it soaked you in sadness that made you never want to feel again. but you will.
- childhood. the second time comes in your twenties, when new cities and lovers bring back that thirst for adventure.
- the stars. they are your guiding light across burning coals and frozen lakes, to the sharpest mountain and the blackest abyss.
- you. you travel, see, love. and then you return home— the little patch of earth where you were once a seed, reaching for the sun.

with a pocketful of stardust

he stumbled alone,
a single surviving star
in the wake of midnight war

his light twinkled faintly
calling for survivors but
only silence echoed back

as his footsteps grew weary
he tumbled into a blackhole
and was swallowed, down

down

down

and he closed his eyes—
giving up, giving in
yet the darkness did not win

from his pockets stardust poured
a billowing tornado of golden hope
rescuing him from endless night

(*the stardust lived within*)

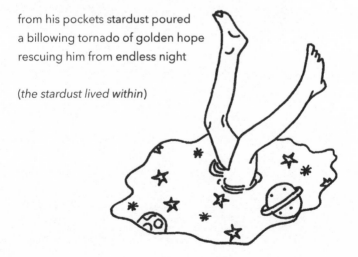

your heart needs
to know how it feels
to be handled badly

if it didn't
how would you know
what you're made of?

(*tough stuff*)

<u>this is how i survive:</u>
- open my petals to the bright blue sky. let the sun scorch me. let storms nourish me.
- find my groove, my pace in the wake of change.
- people. passion. places.
- hold onto hope. always.
- swim in my pool of creativity.
- hunt for new ways to get my heart beating.
- keep this close: everything that is lost is on route to being found.

i know you will be
the string of stars
drawing me a path
out of this darkness

(*oh shooting star*)

once my love had been a wildfire
burning forests to the ground

your eyes reminded me
of that scorching flame

but this time you willed me
to love like a forest not a fire

'be the rain that encourages the seed
be the earth that nourishes the trees'

(*from seed to tree*)

my body sighed
as you shifted closer
electric buzzing in the
fragile space between

your laughter poured
into me like molten
the promise of an
almost intimacy

(*we could light a city, you and i*)

i let my eyes linger
on the curve of his neck
where adam left an apple or
where the moon sits in his eye

(*won't you linger on me?*)

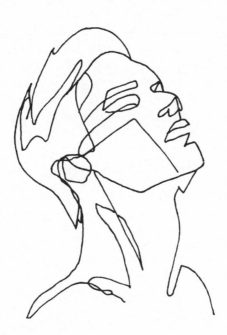

he is my temptation—
one touch to make me hollow
one kiss to make me whole

(*which will it be?*)

<u>questions i have for him:</u>

- how is your skin always so golden? you are the sun and
  i am a star desperately reaching.
- did you hesitate when our hands brushed? did you hear
  the quivering murmur of desire?
- what's the song you sing in the shower? mine is
  'casualty of love.'
- do you like peach ice tea? i bet you'd taste like
  summertime sweetness on my tongue.
- i want to tell you...
- i want you to know...
- do you even notice me?

can i nestle myself
into that soft place
above your heart
and dance along
the embers on
your tongue?

(*our music*)

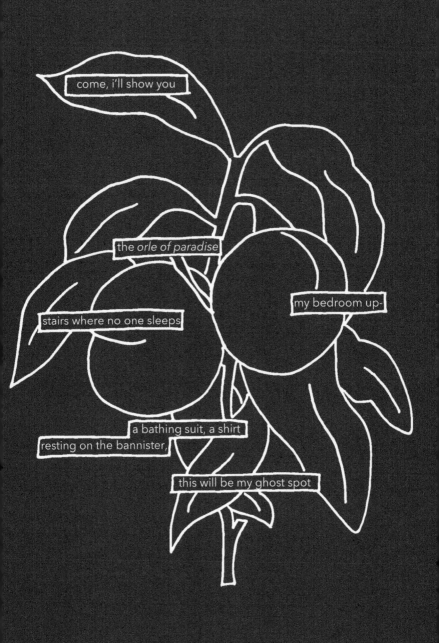

come, i'll show you

the *orle of paradise*

my bedroom up-

stairs where no one sleeps

a bathing suit, a shirt
resting on the bannister,

this will be my ghost spot

you have that warm
symphony of a voice
the kind that weaves
a tapestry of dreams
within me

(*i sing the harmonies*)

i drank him in
the darkest wine
intoxicating my lips
with his silent curse
dressed like a dream

(*hypnotise me*)

take me gently
in your hands
etch me like art
and i will try
to be your
masterpiece

(*our story hangs on the wall of a museum*)

he is sweeter than
homegrown honey
sticking my fingers
to the tips of his own
like he'll never let go

(*sticky sweet*)

you are the sunset
people spend
a little longer
admiring

(*radiate*)

we frame the things
we want to remember
oh please, let me frame
you between my fingers

(*be my gallery*)

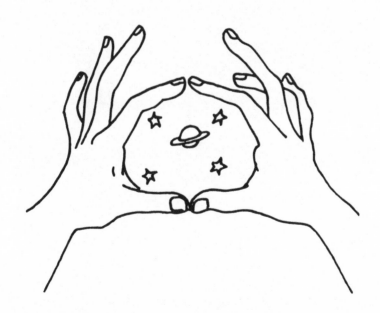

i wrote poetry along
the creases of your hands
told the world how light
tumbles over your knuckles
a twinkle of magic cupped
in your silk soft palms

(*hand in hand*)

darling
if you are
my sunshine
i will try to be
your moonlight
and we'll collide
setting the universe
alight with our love

(*our galaxy*)

<u>what my heart would say:</u>
- i breathe in your laughter, fill my lungs with the warm smoke of you on these cool autumnal nights.
- did electricity tickle your skin when our hands first brushed?
- those icy eyes make my heart pound. let me thaw you.
- i see secrets binding your wrists. share them with me and i will share mine with you.
- no matter where i go, my stars keep drawing a path back to you.

do you see
the stars dancing
across the gaps
between your fingers
and mine?

(*how they flicker*)

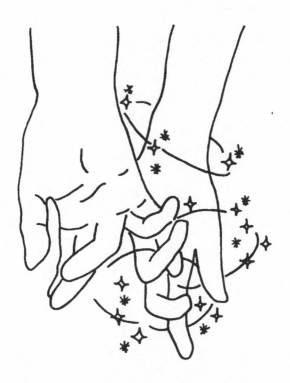

if i am
the sea
you are
the sand
i caress you
gently wash
each grain of
your shores
with my love

(*this poem is the tide*)

i don't need
a lighthouse
when i have
your glow
to guide me

(*bring me home*)

love with you
was inventing a colour
i'd been too blind to see
and too nervous to imagine

(*rainbow boy*)

whisper my name
in the creases of the dark
or under rays of daylight
and i will come running

(*hopelessly devoted*)

i turn to him,
fingers interwoven
and think to myself,
'how could it be
any other way?'

(*two halves of a whole*)

i won't pluck stars
from the night for you
even if you asked me to

i'd put you up there
a star whose beauty
rivals even the moon

(*put you on a pedestal*)

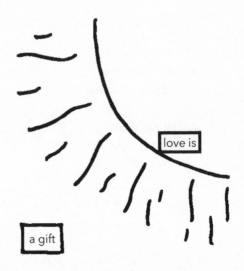

love is

a gift

you become

underneath those skies, your hand
in his

a painting

you

frame

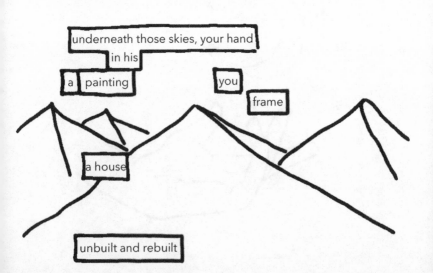

a house

unbuilt and rebuilt

he danced
a constellation

he was a star, yearning
for hands that may hold
his missing piece

he trusted the universe
would navigate him there
to a place called 'found'

but he did not find it
in the hands of another
he painted it with his own

the constellation of him
a landscape of dreams
hung on a lavender sky

(*he is all he needs*)

i nurtured this field of flowers
delicate petals, silently strong

i will not let his thunderstorm
rip through my beauty again

(*you will never uproot me*)

i used to believe my horizons
would turn deep blue without
your hand holding my hand
your eyes holding my eyes

i was wrong

when my hand was dropped
it swayed empty for a while but
soon found solace in my other hand
held it dearer than i ever held yours

(*reliable*)

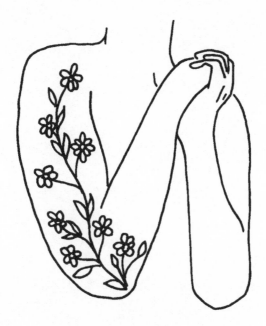

it would have been
easy to turn to stone
as the bruises bloomed
across my delicate skin
but i wear softness
bravely like a medal

(*this fragile rebellion*)

my body is
a glass jar

lightening cracks
along my back

chips where pieces
have fallen away

i have glue here
and here and here

i am as whole
as i want to be

(*broken but whole*)

he was my first love
but i am my second love
and all the loves that follow

(*my own romance*)

<u>how to love yourself:</u>
- take a walk alone. feel the sun caressing your skin, the hum of nature in your ears.
- soothe your body and soul in a bath.
- be bold. get the piercing you've always been too anxious to get.
- clear out the clutter in your mind.
- say 'no' when you deserve more.
- let go of comparisons. you are worth more.
- devour that stack of books.
- create. create. create.
- write all your stings out. like streams of anguish pouring from the tips of your fingers. call it poetry.

i stopped weighing myself
against his new lover and
expectations of strangers

when i started to believe
i outweigh them all in
kindness and love and light

(*the right weight*)

she came for me
rain in one hand
sunlight in the other
a recipe of reconstruction

she scooped up my ashes
bathed my feet in fresh soil
watered with a delicate touch

and on the day that i flowered
when her healing was done
oh, how i begged her to stay

(*mother nature*)

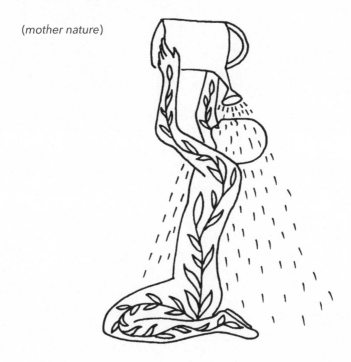

open your arms
to my words for
my survival is
your survival
and my healing
is your healing

(*you are golden*)

<u>when spring comes along:</u>
- dust off the mountains of worry heaped on your shoulders. they have weighed you down.
- the box of trinkets and memories living in your closet must go. it's time for him to go.
- let the sun pour its sweet magic in your soul. with its warmth you will rise.
- throw open the windows to your heart. may a breeze fill your lungs with new love.
- like the forgotten vase on the mantelpiece, you have been empty too long. fill yourself with daffodils, fill yourself with spring.

you will never be too much, never be enough for me... ♡♡♡

LOVE ♡

thank you

TTER THAN
TARRY TRIA[L]
INTO THE CLOUDS

i hope you help me see that love doesn't have to be like it has been for me.

LIKE THE MOON YOU FILL ME WITH. LIKE THE LIGHT ☺ * * *

it's you, you, you, never him, never AGAIN

i ache for the touch of your hand in mine

I ESCAPED THE DARKNES[S]

I WAS

COURA[GEOUS]

i pulled the bars from your cell, so nobody will be held back by you again.

I AM STRONGER NOW

wild with you

THE SCENT OF SUMMER— THE SCENT OF CHANGE!

LOVE

SOFT
SOFT
SOFT
SOFT

SOFTNESS IS POWERFUL

fly like a bird

TREE

NOT
ELSE
HAV
THES
WOR

you wer
in my dre
last night
it u
EUPH

SMILE :)

OR
ME

BLOOM WITHOUT YOU
BLOOM
BLOOM
I
TO LEARNT

Let's set the sky alight together

CH

STRONG

PATH that FEELS right

BE BRAVE BE BOLD

i think i see your eyes up there in the SHAPE of the stars

I
CAN
CAN
CAN
CAN

i'll keep telling myself, i look good today

YOU STRUMMED LIFE BACK INTO ME (OH PLAY ME BABY)

my parents said it first—
'he's sensitive, he's soft'
as if that was an excuse
for my lack of enthusiasm
for football or rugby or
what 'regular' boys did

fast forward ten years and
the narrative stays the same
'don't be so soft,' he scorns
because softness is forbidden

but it is the forbidden fruit i seek
and i have finally found my centre
'i am soft
           i am powerful
                      i am me'

(*soft centre*)

maybe this journey
isn't about becoming
but unbecoming
all that you're not

(*the peeling*)

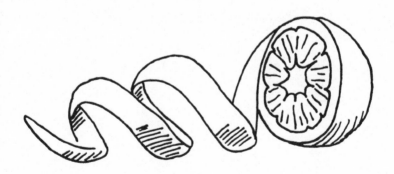

my biggest obstacle
wasn't being lost
but thinking i
couldn't be found

(*i found parts of myself
i never knew existed*)

YOU WILL NEVER ERASE ME

THAT'S LIKE TRYING TO BLOT

STARS FROM THE SKY

(IMPOSSIBLE PAINTER)

let your colours
seep outside the lines
life was not meant
to be lived inside
boundaries

(*breakthrough*)

find people
who help you
breathe deeper
smile brighter
see further
live fuller

(*the ripening*)

if you gaze up and
see no star guiding you
strike your own match
light your own path
through the wilderness

(*yellow brick road*)

the moon calls me
into a forest, shedding
leaves like memories
of the last year and
laying a fiery path
to a new dawn

(*from the ashes*)

reminders:
- you're only twenty-five. you've got time.
- who said you have to be married by thirty?
- don't waste your precious time on toxic people. their poison will make you rot.
- you're going to be okay. trust me.
- worry less. do more.
- stop following their footsteps. pave your own way. leave your own mark.
- speak up. your voice is valid.
- your heart deserves love too.
- stop. smile. take a moment to breathe.

from one constellation to another

about a year ago, a teacher reached out to me to say that my book had helped a boy in her class who was struggling with his sexuality. when i published *this boy is a rainbow*, i had no expectations about who would read it or how it would be received, but i can think of no greater compliment than this.

i'm lucky enough to receive messages of support and solidarity from people every now and then. people who say my words helped them feel less alone or helped them finally let go of a past that had been haunting them. to those people i say this: i am eternally grateful for you and all your love, strength and kindness. your resilience is inspiring.

from time to time, one of you will ask if i'm okay, and the truth is this: maybe, probably, and some days YES. but healing is never linear and i still explore the pain i experienced—the failing and breaking—because it lead me here. i like to think that my survival is the universe's way of offering me a chance to learn, grow, and try again. i will always embrace that.

in this second book, i explore life in my early twenties: that post-adolescent period when finding your place in the universe seems impossible. it is a book about letting go of the past, finding purpose, challenging expectations, struggling with body image and mental health, dating, and learning to love yourself.

above all, this is a book about overcoming not just how other people see you, but how you see yourself. and when you do, learning to celebrate the unique collection of memories and experiences—stars nestled together in the sky—that made your constellation.

i hope this book encourages you to stand up to the blackholes in your universe and find new galaxies of stars that feel right for you. may you burn brighter than the brightest star in the sky.

about the boy

sam payne is a poet and illustrator based in london, uk. after completing his degree in english literature and creative writing, he published his first poetry collection *this boy is a rainbow* in 2018, which tackles first love, heartbreak, and survival.

in his follow-up collection, *this boy is a constellation*, sam takes readers on a journey across the stars as he explores life in his twenties: letting go of the past, finding purpose, challenging expectations, struggling with body image and mental health, dating, and learning to love himself.

when he is not writing, he can be found in a good coffee shop, eating a slice of red velvet cake. you can find out more here: www.bysampayne.com.

Made in the USA
Monee, IL
31 January 2021

59256968R00073